CANZONI & RIPOSTES
OF EZRA POUND

CANZONI & RIPOSTES OF EZRA POUND

EZRA POUND,
THOMAS ERNEST HULME

ISBN: 978-93-5420-545-3

Published: 1913

LECTOR HOUSE LLP
E-MAIL: lectorpublishing@gmail.com

CANZONI & RIPOSTES
OF EZRA POUND

WHERETO ARE APPENDED
THE COMPLETE POETICAL WORKS
OF T. E. HULME

BY

EZRA POUND

MCMXIII

TO
OLIVIA AND DOROTHY SHAKESPEAR

CONTENTS

CONTENTS   vii

RIPOSTES OF EZRA POUND

THE COMPLETE POETICAL WORKS OF T.E. HULME

CANZONI

CANZON: THE YEARLY SLAIN
(WRITTEN IN REPLY TO MANNING'S "KORÈ.")

"Et huiusmodi stantiae usus est fere in omnibus cantionibus suis
Arnaldus Danielis et nos eum secuti sumus."

Dante, *De Vulgari Eloquio*, II. 10.

I

Ah! red-leafed time hath driven out the rose
And crimson dew is fallen on the leaf
Ere ever yet the cold white wheat be sown
That hideth all earth's green and sere and red;
The Moon-flower's fallen and the branch is bare,
Holding no honey for the starry bees;
The Maiden turns to her dark lord's demesne.

II

Fairer than Enna's field when Ceres sows
The stars of hyacinth and puts off grief,
Fairer than petals on May morning blown
Through apple-orchards where the sun hath shed
His brighter petals down to make them fair;
Fairer than these the Poppy-crowned One flees,
And Joy goes weeping in her scarlet train.

III

The faint damp wind that, ere the even, blows
Piling the west with many a tawny sheaf,
Then when the last glad wavering hours are mown
Sigheth and dies because the day is sped;
This wind is like her and the listless air
Wherewith she goeth by beneath the trees,
The trees that mock her with their scarlet stain.

IV

Love that is born of Time and comes and goes!

Love that doth hold all noble hearts in fief!
As red leaves follow where the wind hath flown,
So all men follow Love when Love is dead.
O Fate of Wind! O Wind that cannot spare,
But drivest out the Maid, and pourest lees
Of all thy crimson on the wold again,

V

Korè my heart is, let it stand sans gloze!
Love's pain is long, and lo, love's joy is brief!
My heart erst alway sweet is bitter grown;
As crimson ruleth in the good green's stead,
So grief hath taken all mine old joy's share
And driven forth my solace and all ease
Where pleasure bows to all-usurping pain.

VI

Crimson the hearth where one last ember glows!
My heart's new winter hath no such relief,
Nor thought of Spring whose blossom he hath known
Hath turned him back where Spring is banished.
Barren the heart and dead the fires there,
Blow! O ye ashes, where the winds shall please,
But cry, "Love also is the Yearly Slain."

VII

Be sped, my Canzon, through the bitter air!
To him who speaketh words as fair as these,
Say that I also know the "Yearly Slain."

CANZON: THE SPEAR

I

'Tis the clear light of love I praise
That steadfast gloweth o'er deep waters,
A clarity that gleams always.
Though man's soul pass through troubled waters,
Strange ways to him are openèd.
To shore the beaten ship is sped
If only love of light give aid.

II

That fair far spear of light now lays
Its long gold shaft upon the waters.
Ah! might I pass upon its rays
To where it gleams beyond the waters,
Or might my troubled heart be fed
Upon the frail clear light there shed,
Then were my pain at last allay'd.

III

Although the clouded storm dismays
Many a heart upon these waters,
The thought of that far golden blaze
Giveth me heart upon the waters,
Thinking thereof my bark is led
To port wherein no storm I dread;
No tempest maketh me afraid.

IV

Yet when within my heart I gaze
Upon my fair beyond the waters,
Meseems my soul within me prays
To pass straightway beyond the waters.
Though I be alway banished
From ways and woods that she doth tread,
One thing there is that doth not fade,

V

Deep in my heart that spear-print stays,
That wound I gat beyond the waters,
Deeper with passage of the days
That pass as swift and bitter waters,
While a dull fire within my head
Moveth itself if word be said
Which hath concern with that far maid.

VI

My love is lovelier than the sprays
Of eglantine above clear waters,
Or whitest lilies that upraise
Their heads in midst of moated waters.
No poppy in the May-glad mead
Would match her quivering lips' red
If 'gainst her lips it should be laid.

VII

The light within her eyes, which slays
Base thoughts and stilleth troubled waters,
Is like the gold where sunlight plays
Upon the still o'ershadowed waters.
When anger is there mingled
There comes a keener gleam instead,
Like flame that burns beneath thin jade.

VIII

Know by the words here mingled
What love hath made my heart his stead,
Glowing like flame beneath thin jade.

CANZON: TO BE SUNG BENEATH A WINDOW

I

Heart mine, art mine, whose embraces
Clasp but wind that past thee bloweth
E'en this air so subtly gloweth,
Guerdoned by thy sun-gold traces,
That my heart is half afraid
For the fragrance on him laid;
Even so love's might amazes!

II

Man's love follows many faces,
My love only one face knoweth;
Towards thee only my love floweth,
And outstrips the swift stream's paces.
Were this love well here displayed,
As flame flameth 'neath thin jade
Love should glow through these my phrases.

III

Though I've roamed through many places,
None there is that my heart troweth
Fair as that wherein fair groweth
One whose laud here interlaces
Tuneful words, that I've essayed.
Let this tune be gently played
Which my voice herward upraises.

IV

If my praise her grace effaces,
Then 'tis not my heart that showeth,
But the skilless tongue that soweth
Words unworthy of her graces.
Tongue, that hath me so betrayed,
Were my heart but here displayed,

Then were sung her fitting praises.

CANZON: OF INCENSE

I

Thy gracious ways,
O Lady of my heart, have
O'er all my thought their golden glamour cast;
As amber torch-flames, where strange men-at-arms
Tread softly 'neath the damask shield of night,
Rise from the flowing steel in part reflected,
So on my mailed thought that with thee goeth,
Though dark the way, a golden glamour falleth.

II

The censer sways
And glowing coals some art have
To free what frankincense before held fast
Till all the summer of the eastern farms
Doth dim the sense, and dream up through the light,
As memory, by new-born love corrected—
With savour such as only new love knoweth—
Through swift dim ways the hidden pasts recalleth.

III

On barren days,
At hours when I, apart, have
Bent low in thought of the great charm thou hast,
Behold with music's many-stringed charms
The silence groweth thou. O rare delight!
The melody upon clear strings inflected
Were dull when o'er taut sense thy presence floweth,
With quivering notes' accord that never palleth.

IV

The glowing rays
That from the low sun dart, have
Turned gold each tower and every towering mast;
The saffron flame, that flaming nothing harms
Hides Khadeeth's pearl and all the sapphire might

Of burnished waves, before her gates collected:
The cloak of graciousness, that round thee gloweth,
Doth hide the thing thou art, as here befalleth.

V

All things worth praise
That unto Khadeeth's mart have
From far been brought through perils over-passed,
All santal, myrrh, and spikenard that disarms
The pard's swift anger; these would weigh but light
'Gainst thy delights, my Khadeeth! Whence protected
By naught save her great grace that in him showeth,
My song goes forth and on her mercy calleth.

VI

O censer of the thought that golden gloweth,
Be bright before her when the evening falleth.

VII

Fragrant be thou as a new field one moweth,
O song of mine that "Hers" her mercy calleth.

CANZONE: OF ANGELS

I

He that is Lord of all the realms of light
Hath unto me from His magnificence
Granted such vision as hath wrought my joy.
Moving my spirit past the last defence
That shieldeth mortal things from mightier sight,
Where freedom of the soul knows no alloy,
I saw what forms the lordly powers employ;
Three splendours, saw I, of high holiness,
From clarity to clarity ascending
Through all the roofless, tacit courts extending
In aether which such subtle light doth bless
As ne'er the candles of the stars hath wooed;
Know ye herefrom of their similitude.

II

Withdrawn within the cavern of his wings,
Grave with the joy of thoughts beneficent,
And finely wrought and durable and clear,
If so his eyes showed forth the mind's content,
So sate the first to whom remembrance clings,
Tissued like bat's wings did his wings appear,
Not of that shadowy colouring and drear,
But as thin shells, pale saffron, luminous;
Alone, unlonely, whose calm glances shed
Friend's love to strangers though no word were said,
Pensive his godly state he keepeth thus.
Not with his surfaces his power endeth,
But is as flame that from the gem extendeth.

III

My second marvel stood not in such ease,
But he, the cloudy pinioned, winged him on
Then from my sight as now from memory,
The courier aquiline, so swiftly gone!
The third most glorious of these majesties

Give aid, O sapphires of th' eternal see,
And by your light illume pure verity.
That azure feldspar hight the microcline,
Or, on its wing, the Menelaus weareth
Such subtlety of shimmering as beareth
This marvel onward through the crystalline,
A splendid calyx that about her gloweth,
Smiting the sunlight on whose ray she goeth.

IV

The diver at Sorrento from beneath
The vitreous indigo, who swiftly riseth,
By will and not by action as it seemeth,
Moves not more smoothly, and no thought surmiseth
How she takes motion from the lustrous sheath
Which, as the trace behind the swimmer, gleameth
Yet presseth back the aether where it streameth.
To her whom it adorns this sheath imparteth
The living motion from the light surrounding;
And thus my nobler parts, to grief's confounding,
Impart into my heart a peace which starteth
From one round whom a graciousness is cast
Which clingeth in the air where she hath past.

V—TORNATA

Canzon, to her whose spirit seems in sooth
Akin unto the feldspar, since it is
So clear and subtle and azure, I send thee, saying:
That since I looked upon such potencies
And glories as are here inscribed in truth,
New boldness hath o'erthrown my long delaying,
And that thy words my new-born powers obeying—
Voices at last to voice my heart's long mood—
Are come to greet her in their amplitude.

TO OUR LADY OF VICARIOUS ATONEMENT

(BALLATA)

I

Who are you that the whole world's song
Is shaken out beneath your feet
Leaving you comfortless,
Who, that, as wheat
Is garnered, gather in
The blades of man's sin
And bear that sheaf?
Lady of wrong and grief,
Blameless!

II

All souls beneath the gloom
That pass with little flames,
All these till time be run
Pass one by one
As Christs to save, and die;
What wrong one sowed,
Behold, another reaps!
Where lips awake our joy
The sad heart sleeps
Within.

No man doth bear his sin,
But many sins
Are gathered as a cloud about man's way.

TO GUIDO CAVALCANTI

Dante and I are come to learn of thee,
Ser Guido of Florence, master of us all,
Love, who hath set his hand upon us three,
Bidding us twain upon thy glory call.
Harsh light hath rent from us the golden pall
Of that frail sleep, *His* first light seigniory,
And we are come through all the modes that fall
Unto their lot who meet him constantly.
Wherefore, by right, in this Lord's name we greet thee,
Seeing we labour at his labour daily.
Thou, who dost know what way swift words are crossed
O thou, who hast sung till none at song defeat thee,
Grant! by thy might and hers of San Michele,
Thy risen voice send flames this pentecost.

SONNET IN TENZONE

LA MENTE

"OThou mocked heart that cowerest by the door
And durst not honour hope with welcoming,
How shall one bid thee for her honour sing,
When song would but show forth thy sorrow's store?
What things are gold and ivory unto thee?
Go forth, thou pauper fool! Are these for naught?
Is heaven in lotus leaves? What hast thou wrought,
Or brought, or sought, wherewith to pay the fee?"

IL CUORE

"If naught I give, naught do I take return.
'*Ronsard me celebroit!*' behold I give
The age-old, age-old fare to fairer fair
And I fare forth into more bitter air;
Though mocked I go, yet shall her beauty live
Till rimes unrime and Truth shall truth unlearn."

SONNET: CHI È QUESTA?

Who is she coming, that the roses bend
    Their shameless heads to do her passing honour?
Who is she coming with a light upon her
Not born of suns that with the day's end end?
Say is it Love who hath chosen the nobler part?
Say is it Love, that was divinity,
Who hath left his godhead that his home might be
The shameless rose of her unclouded heart?
If this be Love, where hath he won such grace?
If this be Love, how is the evil wrought,
That all men write against his darkened name?
If this be Love, if this ...
O mind give place!
What holy mystery e'er was noosed in thought?
Own that thou scan'st her not, nor count it shame!

BALLATA, FRAGMENT

II

Full well thou knowest, song, what grace I mean,
E'en as thou know'st the sunlight I have lost.
Thou knowest the way of it and know'st the sheen
About her brows where the rays are bound and crossed,
E'en as thou knowest joy and know'st joy's bitter cost.
Thou know'st her grace in moving,
Thou dost her skill in loving,
Thou know'st what truth she proveth,
Thou knowest the heart she moveth,
O song where grief assoneth!

CANZON: THE VISION

I

When first I saw thee 'neath the silver mist,
    Ruling thy bark of painted sandal-wood,
Did any know thee? By the golden sails
That clasped the ribbands of that azure sea,
Did any know thee save my heart alone?
O ivory woman with thy bands of gold,
Answer the song my luth and I have brought thee!

II

Dream over golden dream that secret cist,
Thy heart, O heart of me, doth hold, and mood
On mood of silver, when the day's light fails,
Say who hath touched the secret heart of thee,
Or who hath known what my heart hath not known
O slender pilot whom the mists enfold,
Answer the song my luth and I have wrought thee!

III

When new love plucks the falcon from his wrist,
And cuts the gyve and casts the scarlet hood,
Where is the heron heart whom flight avails?
O quick to prize me Love, how suddenly
From out the tumult truth has ta'en his own,
And in this vision is our past unrolled.
Lo! With a hawk of light thy love hath caught me.

IV

And I shall get no peace from eucharist,
Nor doling out strange prayers before the rood,
To match the peace that thine hands' touch entails;
Nor doth God's light match light shed over me
When thy caught sunlight is about me thrown,
Oh, for the very ruth thine eyes have told,
Answer the rune this love of thee hath taught me.

V

After an age of longing had we missed
Our meeting and the dream, what were the good
Of weaving cloth of words? Were jewelled tales
An opiate meet to quell the malady
Of life unlived? In untried monotone
Were not the earth as vain, and dry, and old,
For thee, O Perfect Light, had I not sought thee?

VI

Calais, in song where word and tone keep tryst
Behold my heart, and hear mine hardihood!
Calais, the wind is come and heaven pales
And trembles for the love of day to be.
Calais, the words break and the dawn is shown.
Ah, but the stars set when thou wast first bold,
Turn! lest they say a lesser light distraught thee.

VII

O ivory thou, the golden scythe hath mown
Night's stubble and my joy. Thou royal souled,
Favour the quest! Lo, Truth and I have sought thee

OCTAVE

Fine songs, fair songs, these golden usuries
Her beauty earns as but just increment,
And they do speak with a most ill intent
Who say they give when they pay debtor's fees.

I call him bankrupt in the courts of song
Who hath her gold to eye and pays her not,
Defaulter do I call the knave who hath got
Her silver in his heart, and doth her wrong.

SONNET: THE TALLY-BOARD

If on the tally-board of wasted days
They daily write me for proud idleness,
Let high Hell summons me, and I confess,
No overt act the preferred charge allays.

To-day I thought—what boots it what I thought?
Poppies and gold! Why should I blurt it out?
Or hawk the magic of her name about
Deaf doors and dungeons where no truth is bought?

Who calls me idle? I have thought of her.
Who calls me idle? By God's truth I've seen
The arrowy sunlight in her golden snares.

Let him among you all stand summonser
Who hath done better things! Let whoso hath been
With worthier works concerned, display his wares!

BALLATETTA

The light became her grace and dwelt among
Blind eyes and shadows that are formed as men
Lo, how the light doth melt us into song:

The broken sunlight for a healm she beareth
Who hath my heart in jurisdiction.
In wild-wood never fawn nor fallow fareth
So silent light; no gossamer is spun
So delicate as she is, when the sun
Drives the clear emeralds from the bended grasses
Lest they should parch too swiftly, where she passes.

MADRIGALE

C lear is my love but shadowed
By the spun gold above her,
Ah, what a petal those bent sheaths discover!

The olive wood hath hidden her completely.
She was gowned that discreetly
The leaves and shadows concealed her completely.

Fair is my love but followed
In all her goings surely
By gracious thoughts, she goeth so demurely.

ERA MEA

Era mea
In qua terra
Dulce myrti floribus,
Rosa amoris
Via erroris
Ad te coram
Veniam?

ANGLICÈ REDDITA

Mistress mine, in what far land,
Where the myrtle bloweth sweet
Shall I weary with my way-fare,
Win to thee that art as day fair,
Lay my roses at thy feet?

THRENOS

No more for us the little sighing,
No more the winds at twilight trouble us.

Lo the fair dead!

No more do I burn.
No more for us the fluttering of wings
That whirred in the air above us.

Lo the fair dead!

No more desire flayeth me,
No more for us the trembling
At the meeting of hands.

Lo the fair dead!

No more for us the wine of the lips,
No more for us the knowledge.

Lo the fair dead!

No more the torrent,
No more for us the meeting-place
(Lo the fair dead!)
Tintagoel.

THE TREE

I stood still and was a tree amid the wood,
Knowing the truth of things unseen before;
Of Daphne and the laurel bow
And that god-feasting couple old
That grew elm-oak amid the wold.
'Twas not until the gods had been
Kindly entreated, and been brought within
Unto the hearth of their heart's home
That they might do this wonder thing;
Nathless I have been a tree amid the wood
And many a new thing understood
That was rank folly to my head before.

PARACELSUS IN EXCELSIS

"Being no longer human why should I
Pretend humanity or don the frail attire?
Men have I known, and men, but never one
Was grown so free an essence, or become
So simply element as what I am.
The mist goes from the mirror and I see!
Behold! the world of forms is swept beneath—
Turmoil grown visible beneath our peace,
And we, that are grown formless, rise above—
Fluids intangible that have been men,
We seem as statues round whose high-risen base
Some overflowing river is run mad,
In us alone the element of calm!"

DE AEGYPTO

I even I, am he who knoweth the roads
Through the sky, and the wind thereof is my body.

I have beheld the Lady of Life,
I, even I, who fly with the swallows.

Green and gray is her raiment,
Trailing along the wind.

I, even I, am he who knoweth the roads
Through the sky, and the wind thereof is my body.

Manus animam pinxit,
My pen is in my hand

To write the acceptable word....
My mouth to chant the pure singing!

Who hath the mouth to receive it,
The song of the Lotus of Kumi?

I, even I, am he who knoweth the roads
Through the sky, and the wind thereof is my body.

I am flame that riseth in the sun,
I, even I, who fly with the swallows.

The moon is upon my forehead,
The winds are under my lips.

The moon is a great pearl in the waters of sapphire,
Cool to my fingers the flowing waters.

I, even I, am he who knoweth the roads
Through the sky, and the wind thereof is my body.

I will return to the halls of the flowing,
Of the truth of the children of Ashu.

I, even I, am he who knoweth the roads
Of the sky, and the wind thereof is my body.

LI BEL CHASTEUS

That castle stands the highest in the land
Far seen and mighty. Of the great hewn stones
What shall I say? And deep foss way
That far beneath us bore of old
A swelling turbid sea
Hill-born and tumultuous
Unto the fields below, where
Staunch villein and
Burgher held the land and tilled
Long labouring for gold of wheat grain
And to see the beards come forth
For barley's even time.

But archèd high above the curl of life
We dwelt amid the ancient boulders,
Gods had hewn and druids turned
Unto that birth most wondrous, that had grown
A mighty fortress while the world had slept,
And we awaited in the shadows there
When mighty hands had laboured sightlessly
And shaped this wonder 'bove the ways of men.
Me seems we could not see the great green waves
Nor rocky shore by Tintagoel
From this our hold,
But came faint murmuring as undersong,
E'en as the burghers' hum arose
And died as faint wind melody
Beneath our gates.

PRAYER FOR HIS LADY'S LIFE
FROM PROPERTIUS, ELEGIAE, LIB. III, 26

Here let thy clemency, Persephone, hold firm,
Do thou, Pluto, bring here no greater harshness.
So many thousand beauties are gone down to Avernus
Ye might let one remain above with us.

With you is Iope, with you the white-gleaming Tyro,
With you is Europa and the shameless Pasiphae,
And all the fair from Troy and all from Achaia,
From the sundered realms, of Thebes and of aged Priamus;
And all the maidens of Rome, as many as they were,
They died and the greed of your flame consumes them.

Here let thy clemency, Persephone, hold firm,
Do thou, Pluto, bring here no greater harshness.
So many thousand fair are gone down to Avernus,
Ye might let one remain above with us.

SPEECH FOR PSYCHE IN THE GOLDEN BOOK OF APULEIUS

All night, and as the wind lieth among
The cypress trees, he lay,
Nor held me save as air that brusheth by one
Close, and as the petals of flowers in falling
Waver and seem not drawn to earth, so he
Seemed over me to hover light as leaves
And closer me than air,
And music flowing through me seemed to open
Mine eyes upon new colours.
O winds, what wind can match the weight of him!

"BLANDULA, TENULLA, VAGULA."

What hast thou, O my soul, with paradise?
Will we not rather, when our freedom's won,
Get us to some clear place wherein the sun
Lets drift in on us through the olive leaves
A liquid glory? If at Sirmio
My soul, I meet thee, when this life's outrun,
Will we not find some headland consecrated
By aery apostles of terrene delight,
Will not our cult be founded on the waves,
Clear sapphire, cobalt, cyanine,
On triune azures, the impalpable
Mirrors unstill of the eternal change?

Soul, if She meet us there, will any rumour
Of havens more high and courts desirable
Lure us beyond the cloudy peak of Riva?

ERAT HORA

"Thank you, whatever comes." And then she turned
And, as the ray of sun on hanging flowers
Fades when the wind hath lifted them aside,
Went swiftly from me. Nay, whatever comes
One hour was sunlit and the most high gods
May not make boast of any better thing
Than to have watched that hour as it passed.

EPIGRAMS

I

O ivory, delicate hands!
O face that hovers
Between "To-come" and "Was,"
Ivory thou wast,
A rose thou wilt be.

II
(THE SEA OF GLASS)

I looked and saw a sea roofed over with rainbows,
In the midst of each two lovers met and departed;
Then the sky was full of faces with gold glories behind them.

LA NUVOLETTA

"Dante to an unknown lady, beseeching her not to interrupt
his cult of the dead Beatrice. From "Il Canzoniere," Ballata II.

Ah little cloud that in Love's shadow lief
Upon mine eyes so suddenly alightest,
Take some faint pity on the heart thou smitest
That hopes in thee, desires, dies, in brief.

Ah little cloud of more than human fashion
Thou settest a flame within my mind's mid space
With thy deathly speech that grieveth;

Then as a fiery spirit in thy ways
Createst hope, in part a rightful passion,
Yet where thy sweet smile giveth
His grace, look not! For in Her my faith liveth.

Think on my high desire whose flame's so great
That nigh a thousand who were come too late,
Have felt the torment of another's grief.

ROSA SEMPITERNA

A rose I set within my "Paradise"
Lo how his red is turned to yellowness,
Not withered but grown old in subtler wise
Between the empaged rime's high holiness
Where Dante sings of that rose's device
Which yellow is, with souls in blissfulness.
Rose whom I set within my paradise,
Donor of roses and of parching sighs,
Of golden lights and dark unhappiness,
Of hidden chains and silvery joyousness,
Hear how thy rose within my Dante lies,
O rose I set within my paradise.

THE GOLDEN SESTINA

FROM THE ITALIAN OF PICO DELLA MIRANDOLA

In the bright season when He, most high Jove,
From welkin reaching down his glorying hand,
Decks the Great Mother and her changing face,
Clothing her not with scarlet skeins and gold
But with th' empurpling flowers and gay grass,
When the young year renewed, renews the sun,

When, then, I see a lady like the sun,
One fashioned by th' high hand of utmost Jove,
So fair beneath the myrtles on gay grass
Who holdeth Love and Truth, one by each hand,
It seems, if I look straight, two bands of gold
Do make more fair her delicate fair face.

Though eyes are dazzled, looking on her face
As all sight faileth that looks toward the sun,
New metamorphoses, to rained gold,
Or bulls or whitest swans, might fall on Jove
Through her, or Phoebus, his bag-pipes in hand,
Might, mid the droves, come barefoot o'er our grass,

Alas, that there was hidden in the grass
A cruel shaft, the which, to wound my face,
My Lady took in her own proper hand.
If I could not defend me 'gainst that sun
I take no shame, for even utmost Jove
Is in high heaven pierced with darts of gold.

Behold the green shall find itself turned gold
And spring shall be without her flowers and grass,
And hell's deep be the dwelling place of Jove
Ere I shall have uncarved her holy face
From my heart's midst, where 'tis both Sun and sun
And yet she beareth me such hostile hand!

O sweet and holy and O most light hand,
O intermingled ivory and gold,
O mortal goddess and terrestrial sun
Who comest not to foster meadow grass,

But to show heaven by a likened face
Wert sent amongst us by th' exalted Jove,

I still pray Jove that he permit no grass
To cover o'er thy hands, thy face, thy gold
For heaven's sufficed with a single sun.

ROME (FROM DU BELLAY)
FROM THE FRENCH OF JOACHIM DU BELLAY

"Troica Roma resurges."

PROPERTIUS.

O thou new comer who seek'st Rome in Rome
And find'st in Rome no thing thou canst call Roman;
Arches worn old and palaces made common,
Rome's name alone within these walls keeps home.

Behold how pride and ruin can befall
One who hath set the whole world 'neath her laws,
All-conquering, now conquered, because
She is Time's prey and Time consumeth all.

Rome that art Rome's one sole last monument,
Rome that alone hast conquered Rome the town,
Tiber alone, transient and seaward bent,
Remains of Rome. O world, thou unconstant mime!
That which stands firm in thee Time batters down,
And that which fleeteth doth outrun swift time.

HER MONUMENT,
THE IMAGE CUT THEREON

FROM THE ITALIAN OF LEOPARDI

(Written 1831-3 circa)

Such wast thou,
Who art now
But buried dust and rusted skeleton.
Above the bones and mire,
Motionless, placed in vain,
Mute mirror of the flight of speeding years,
Sole guard of grief
Sole guard of memory
Standeth this image of the beauty sped.

O glance, when thou wast still as thou art now,
How hast thou set the fire
A-tremble in men's veins; O lip curved high
To mind me of some urn of full delight,
O throat girt round of old with swift desire,
O palms of Love, that in your wonted ways
Not once but many a day
Felt hands turn ice a-sudden, touching ye,
That ye were once! of all the grace ye had
That which remaineth now
Shameful, most sad
Finds 'neath this rock fit mould, fit resting place!

And still when fate recalleth,
Even that semblance that appears amongst us
Is like to heaven's most 'live imagining.
All, all our life's eternal mystery!
To-day, on high
Mounts, from our mighty thoughts and from the fount
Of sense untellable, Beauty
That seems to be some quivering splendour cast
By the immortal nature on this quicksand,
And by surhuman fates

Given to mortal state
To be a sign and an hope made secure
Of blissful kingdoms and the aureate spheres;
And on the morrow, by some lightsome twist,
Shameful in sight, abject, abominable
All this angelic aspect can return
And be but what it was
With all the admirable concepts that moved from it
Swept from the mind with it in its departure.

Infinite things desired, lofty visions
'Got on desirous thought by natural virtue,
And the wise concord, whence through delicious seas
The arcane spirit of the whole Mankind
Turns hardy pilot ... and if one wrong note
Strike the tympanum,
Instantly
That paradise is hurled to nothingness.

O mortal nature,
If thou art
Frail and so vile in all,
How canst thou reach so high with thy poor sense;
Yet if thou art
Noble in any part
How is the noblest of thy speech and thought
So lightly wrought
Or to such base occasion lit and quenched?

VICTORIAN ECLOGUES

I
EXCUSES

Ah would you turn me back now from the flowers,
You who are different as the air from sea is,
Ah for the pollen from our wreath of hours,
You who are magical, not mine as she is,
Say will you call us from our time of flowers?

You whom I loved and love, not understanding,
Yea we were ever torn with constant striving,
Seeing our gods are different, and commanding
One good from them, and in my heart reviving
Old discords and bent thought, not understanding.

We who have wept, we who have lain together
Upon the green and sere and white of every season,
We who have loved the sun but for the weather
Of our own hearts have found no constant reason,
What is your part, now we have come together?

What is your pain, Dear, what is your heart now
A little sad, a little.... Nay, I know not
Seeing I never had and have no part now
In your own secret councils wherein blow not
My roses. My vineyard being another heart now?

You who were ever dear and dearer being strange,
How shall I "go" who never came anear you?
How could I stay, who never came in range
Of anything that halved; could never hear you
Rightly in your silence; nay, your very speech was strange.

You, who have loved not what I was or will be,
You who but loved me for a thing I could be,
You who love not a song whate'er its skill be
But only love the cause or what cause should be,
How could I give you what I am or will be?

Nay, though your eyes are sad, you will not hinder,
You, who would have had me only near not nearer,

Nay though my heart had burned to a bright cinder
Love would have said to me: "Still fear her,
Pain is thy lot and naught she hath can hinder,"

So I, for this sad gladness that is mine now,
Who never spoke aright in speaking to you,
Uncomprehending anything that's thine now,
E'en in my spoken words more wrong may do you
In looking back from this new grace that's mine now.

Sic semper finis deest.

II
SATIEMUS

What if I know thy speeches word by word?
　　And if thou knew'st I knew them wouldst thou speak?
What if I know thy speeches word by word,
And all the time thou sayest them o'er I said,
"Lo, one there was who bent her fair bright head,
Sighing as thou dost through the golden speech."
Or, as our laughters mingle each with each,
As crushed lips take their respite fitfully,
What if my thoughts were turned in their mid reach
Whispering among them, "The fair dead
Must know such moments, thinking on the grass;
On how white dogwoods murmured overhead
In the bright glad days!"
How if the low dear sound within thy throat
Hath as faint lute-strings in its dim accord
Dim tales that blind me, running one by one
With times told over as we tell by rote;
What if I know thy laughter word by word
Nor find aught novel in thy merriment?

III
ABELARD

"*Pere Esbaillart a Sanct Denis.*"

VILLON.

"Because my soul cried out, and only the long ways
　Grown weary, gave me answer and
Because she answered when the very ways were dumb
With all their hoarse, dry speech grown faint and chill.
Because her answer was a call to me,
Though I have sinned, my God, and though thy angels
Bear no more now my thought to whom I love;
Now though I crouch afraid in all thy dark

Will I once cry to thee:
Once more! Once more my strength!
Yea though I sin to call him forth once more,
Thy messengers for mine, Their wings my power!
And let once more my wings fold down above her,
Let their cool length be spread
Over her feet and head
And let thy calm come down
To dwell within her, and thy gown of peace
Clothe all her body in its samite.
O Father of all the blind and all the strong,
Though I have left thy courts, though all the throng
Of thy gold-shimmering choir know me not,
Though I have dared the body and have donned
Its frail strong-seeming, and although
Its lightening joy is made my swifter song,
Though I have known thy stars, yea all, and chosen one.
Yea though I make no barter, and repent no jot,
Yet for the sunlight of that former time
Grant me the boon, O God,
Once more, once more, or I or some white thought
Shall rise beside her and, enveloping
All her strange glory in its wings of light,
Bring down thy peace upon her way-worn soul.
Oh sheathe that sword of her in some strong case,
The doe-skin scabbard of thy clear Rafael!
Yea let thy angels walk, as I have seen
Them passing, or have seen their wings
Spread their pavilions o'er our twin delight.
Yea I have seen them when the purple light
Hid all her garden from my drowsy eyes.

A PROLOGUE

SCENE—IN THE AIR

The Lords of the Air:

What light hath passed us in the silent ways?
The Spirits of Fire:

We are sustainèd, strengthened suddenly.

The Spirits of Water:

Lo, how the utmost deeps are clarified!

The Spirits Terrene:

What might is this more potent than the spring?
Lo, how the night
Which wrapped us round with its most heavy cloths
Opens and breathes with some strange-fashioned brighness!

IN HEAVEN

Christ, the eternal Spirit in Heaven speaketh thus, over the child of Mary:

O star, move forth and write upon the skies,
"This child is born in ways miraculous."

* * * * *

O windy spirits, that are born in Heaven,
Go down and bid the powers of Earth and Air
Protect his ways until the Time shall come.

* * * * *

O Mother, if the dark of things to be
Wrap round thy heart with cloudy apprehensions,
Eat of thy present corn, the aftermath
Hath its appointed end in whirling light.
Eat of thy present corn, thou so hast share
In mightier portents than Augustus hath.

* * * * *

In every moment all to be is born,
Thou art the moment and need'st fear no scorn.

Echo of the Angels singing "Exultasti":

> Silence is born of many peaceful things,
> Thus is the starlight woven into strings
> Whereon the Powers of peace make sweet accord.
> Rejoice, O Earth, thy Lord
> Hath chosen Him his holy resting-place.
>
> Lo, how the winged sign
> Flutters above that hallowed chrysalis.

IN THE AIR

The invisible Spirit of the Star answers them:

> Bend in your singing, gracious potencies,
> Bend low above your ivory bows and gold!
> That which ye know but dimly hath been wrought
> High in the luminous courts and azure ways:
> Bend in your praise;
> For though your subtle thought
> Sees but in part the source of mysteries,
> Yet are ye bidden in your songs, sing this:
>
> > *"Gloria! gloria in excelsis*
> > *Pax in terra nunc natast."*

Angels continuing in song:

> Shepherds and kings, with lambs and frankincense
> Go and atone for mankind's ignorance:
> Make ye soft savour from your ruddy myrrh.
> Lo, how God's son is turned God's almoner.
> Give ye this little
> Ere he give ye all.

ON EARTH

One of the Magi:

> How the deep-voicèd night turns councillor!
> And how, for end, our starry meditations
> Admit us to his board!

A Shepherd:

> Sir, we be humble and perceive ye are
> Men of great power and authority,
> And yet we too have heard.

DIANA IN EPHESUS

(Lucina dolentibus:)

> "Behold the deed! Behold the act supreme!

With mine own hands have I prepared my doom,
Truth shall grow great eclipsing other truth,
And men forget me in the aging years."

Explicit.

MAESTRO DI TOCAR

(W.R.)

You, who are touched not by our mortal ways
  Nor girded with the stricture of our bands,
Have but to loose the magic from your hands
And all men's hearts that glimmer for a day,
And all our loves that are so swift to flame
Rise in that space of sound and melt away.

ARIA

My love is a deep flame that hides beneath the waters.
—My love is gay and kind,
My love is hard to find as the flame beneath the waters.

The fingers of the wind meet hers
With a frail swift greeting.
My love is gay and kind and hard of meeting,
As the flame beneath the waters hard of meeting.

L'ART

When brightest colours seem but dull in hue
And noblest arts are shown mechanical,
When study serves but to heap clue on clue
That no great line hath been or ever shall,
But hath a savour like some second stew
Of many pot-lots with a smack of all.
'Twas one man's field, another's hops the brew,
Twas vagrant accident not fate's fore-call.
Horace, that thing of thine is overhauled,
And "Wood notes wild" weaves a concocted sonnet.
Here aery Shelley on the text hath called,
And here, Great Scott, the Murex, Keats comes on it.
And all the lot howl, "Sweet Simplicity!"
'Tis Art to hide our theft exquisitely.

SONG IN THE MANNER OF HOUSMAN

O Woe, woe,
People are born and die,
We also shall be dead pretty soon
Therefore let us act as if we were dead already.

The bird sits on the hawthorn tree
But he dies also, presently.
Some lads get hung, and some get shot.
Woeful is this human lot.
Woe! woe, etcetera....

London is a woeful place,
Shropshire is much pleasanter.
Then let us smile a little space
Upon fond nature's morbid grace.
Oh, Woe, woe, woe, etcetera....

TRANSLATIONS FROM HEINE
VON "DIE HEIMKEHR"

I

Is your hate, then, of such measure?
Do you, truly, so detest me?
Through all the world will I complain
Of *how* you have addressed me.

O ye lips that are ungrateful,
Hath it never once distressed you,
That you can say such *awful* things
Of *any* one who ever kissed you?

II

So thou hast forgotten fully
That I so long held thy heart wholly,
Thy little heart, so sweet and false and small
That there's no thing more sweet or false at all.

Love and lay thou hast forgotten fully,
And my heart worked at them unduly.
I know not if the love or if the lay were better stuff,
But I know now, they both were good enough.

III

Tell me where thy lovely love is,
Whom thou once did sing so sweetly,
When the fairy flames enshrouded
Thee, and held thy heart completely.

All the flames are dead and sped now
And my heart is cold and sere;
Behold this book, the urn of ashes,
'Tis my true love's sepulchre.

IV

I dreamt that I was God Himself
Whom heavenly joy immerses,
And all the angels sat about
And praised my verses.

V

The mutilated choir boys
     When I begin to sing
Complain about the awful noise
And call my voice too thick a thing.

When light their voices lift them up,
Bright notes against the ear,
Through trills and runs like crystal,
Ring delicate and clear.

They sing of Love that's grown desirous,
Of Love, and joy that is Love's inmost part,
And all the ladies swim through tears
Toward such a work of art.

VI

This delightful young man
     Should not lack for honourers,
He propitiates me with oysters,
With Rhine wine and liqueurs.

How his coat and pants adorn him!
Yet his ties are more adorning,
In these he daily comes to ask me:
Are you feeling well this morning?

He speaks of my extended fame,
My wit, charm, definitions,
And is diligent to serve me,
Is detailed in his provisions.

In evening company he sets his face
In most spiritu*el* positions,
And declaims before the ladies
My *god-like* compositions.

O what comfort is it for me
To find him such, when the days bring
No comfort, at my time of life when
All good things go vanishing.

TRANSLATOR TO TRANSLATED

O Harry Heine, curses be,
I live too late to sup with thee!
Who can demolish at such polished ease
Philistia's pomp and Art's pomposities!

VII

SONG FROM DIE HARZREISE.

I am the Princess Ilza
In Ilsenstein I fare,
Come with me to that castle
And we'll be happy there.

Thy head will I cover over
With my waves' clarity
Till thou forget thy sorrow,
O wounded sorrowfully.

Thou wilt in my white arms there,
Nay, on my breast thou must
Forget and rest and dream there
For thine old legend-lust.

My lips and my heart are thine there
As they were his and mine.
His? Why the good King Harry's,
And he is dead lang syne.

Dead men stay alway dead men,
Life is the live man's part,
And I am fair and golden
With joy breathless at heart.

If my heart stay below there,
My crystal halls ring clear
To the dance of lords and ladies
In all their splendid gear.

The silken trains go rustling,
The spur-clinks sound between,
The dark dwarfs blow and bow there
Small horn and violin.

Yet shall my white arms hold thee,
That bound King Harry about.
Ah, I covered his ears with them
When the trumpet rang out.

UND DRANG

Nay, dwells he in cloudy rumour alone?

BINYON.

I

I am worn faint,
The winds of good and evil
Blind me with dust
And burn me with the cold,
There is no comfort being over-man;
Yet are we come more near
The great oblivions and the labouring night,
Inchoate truth and the sepulchral forces.

II

Confusion, clamour, 'mid the many voices
Is there a meaning, a significance?

That life apart from all life gives and takes,
This life, apart from all life's bitter and life's sweet,
Is good.

Ye see me and ye say: exceeding sweet
Life's gifts, his youth, his art,
And his too soon acclaim.

I also knew exceeding bitterness,
Saw good things altered and old friends fare forth,
And what I loved in me hath died too soon,
Yea I have seen the "gray above the green";
Gay have I lived in life;
Though life hath lain
Strange hands upon me and hath torn my sides,
Yet I believe.

*   *   *   *   *

Life is most cruel where she is most wise.

III

The will to live goes from me. I have lain
Dull and out-worn with some strange, subtle sickness.
Who shall say
That love is not the very root of this,
O thou afar?

Yet she was near me, that eternal deep.
O it is passing strange that love
Can blow two ways across one soul.
*   *   *   *   *

And I was Aengus for a thousand years,
And she, the ever-living, moved with me
And strove amid the waves, and would not go.

IV

ELEGIA

"Far buon tempo e trionfare"

"I have put my days and dreams out of mind'
For all their hurry and their weary fret
Availed me little. But another kind
Of leaf that's fast in some more sombre wind,
Is man on life, and all our tenuous courses
Wind and unwind as vainly.
*   *   *   *   *

I have lived long, and died,
Yea I have been dead, right often,
And have seen one thing:
The sun, while he is high, doth light our wrong
And none can break the darkness with a song.

To-day's the cup. To-morrow is not ours:
Nay, by our strongest bands we bind her not,
Nor all our fears and our anxieties
Turn her one leaf or hold her scimitar.

The deed blots out the thought
And many thoughts, the vision;
And right's a compass with as many poles
As there are points in her circumference,
'Tis vain to seek to steer all courses even,
And all things save sheer right are vain enough.
The blade were vain to grow save toward the sun,
And vain th' attempt to hold her green forever.

All things in season and no thing o'er long!

Love and desire and gain and good forgetting,
Thou canst not stay the wheel, hold none too long!

V

How our modernity,
Nerve-wracked and broken, turns
Against time's way and all the way of things,
Crying with weak and egoistic cries!
*　　　*　　　*　　　*　　　*

All things are given over,
Only the restless will
Surges amid the stars
Seeking new moods of life,
New permutations.
*　　　*　　　*　　　*　　　*

See, and the very sense of what we know
Dodges and hides as in a sombre curtain
Bright threads leap forth, and hide, and leave no pattern.

VI

I thought I had put Love by for a time
And I was glad, for to me his fair face
Is like Pain's face.
A little light,
The lowered curtain and the theatre!
And o'er the frail talk of the inter-act
Something that broke the jest! A little light,
The gold, and half the profile!
The whole face
Was nothing like you, yet that image cut
Sheer through the moment.

VI*b*

I have gone seeking for you in the twilight,
Here in the flurry of Fifth Avenue,
Here where they pass between their teas and teas.
Is it such madness? though you could not be
Ever in all that crowd, no gown
Of all their subtle sorts could be your gown.

Yet I am fed with faces, is there one
That even in the half-light mindeth me.

VII

THE HOUSE OF SPLENDOUR

'Tis Evanoe's,
  A house not made with hands,
But out somewhere beyond the worldly ways
Her gold is spread, above, around, inwoven,
Strange ways and walls are fashioned out of it.

And I have seen my Lady in the sun,
Her hair was spread about, a sheaf of wings,
And red the sunlight was, behind it all.

And I have seen her there within her house,
With six great sapphires hung along the wall,
Low, panel-shaped, a-level with her knees,
And all her robe was woven of pale gold.

There are there many rooms and all of gold,
Of woven walls deep patterned, of email,
Of beaten work; and through the claret stone,
Set to some weaving, comes the aureate light.

Here am I come perforce my love of her,
Behold mine adoration
Maketh me clear, and there are powers in this
Which, played on by the virtues of her soul,
Break down the four-square walls of standing time.

VIII

THE FLAME

'Tis not a game that plays at mates and mating,
  Provençe knew;
'Tis not a game of barter, lands and houses,
Provençe knew.
We who are wise beyond your dream of wisdom,
Drink our immortal moments; we "pass through."
We have gone forth beyond your bonds and borders,
Provençe knew;
And all the tales they ever writ of Oisin
Say but this:
That man doth pass the net of days and hours.
Where time is shrivelled down to time's seed corn
We of the Ever-living, in that light
Meet through our veils and whisper, and of love.

O smoke and shadow of a darkling world,
Barters of passion, and that tenderness
That's but a sort of cunning! O my Love,

These, and the rest, and all the rest we knew.

'Tis not a game that plays at mates and mating,
'Tis not a game of barter, lands and houses,
'Tis not "of days and nights" and troubling years,
Of cheeks grown sunken and glad hair gone gray;
There *is* the subtler music, the clear light

Where time burns back about th' eternal embers.
We are not shut from all the thousand heavens:
Lo, there are many gods whom we have seen,
Folk of unearthly fashion, places splendid,
Bulwarks of beryl and of chrysophrase.

Sapphire Benacus, in thy mists and thee
Nature herself's turned metaphysical,
Who can look on that blue and not believe?

Thou hooded opal, thou eternal pearl,
O thou dark secret with a shimmering floor,
Through all thy various mood I know thee mine;

If I have merged my soul, or utterly
Am solved and bound in, through aught here on earth,
There canst thou find me, O thou anxious thou,
Who call'st about my gates for some lost me;
I say my soul flowed back, became translucent.
Search not my lips, O Love, let go my hands,
This thing that moves as man is no more mortal.
If thou hast seen my shade sans character,
If thou hast seen that mirror of all moments,
That glass to all things that o'ershadow it,
Call not that mirror me, for I have slipped
Your grasp, I have eluded.

IX

(HORAE BEATAE INSCRIPTIO)

How will this beauty, when I am far hence,
Sweep back upon me and engulf my mind!

How will these hours, when we twain are gray,
Turned in their sapphire tide, come flooding o'er us!

X

(THE ALTAR)

Let us build here an exquisite friendship,
The flame, the autumn, and the green rose of love
Fought out their strife here, 'tis a place of wonder;
Where these have been, meet 'tis, the ground is holy.

IX

(AU SALON)

Her grave, sweet haughtiness
Pleaseth me, and in like wise
Her quiet ironies.
Others are beautiful, none more, some less.

I suppose, when poetry comes down to facts,
When our souls are returned to the gods and the spheres they belong in,
Here in the every-day where our acts
Rise up and judge us;

I suppose there are a few dozen verities
That no shift of mood can shake from us:

One place where we'd rather have tea
(Thus far hath modernity brought us)
"Tea" (Damn you!)
Have tea, damn the Caesars,
Talk of the latest success, give wing to some scandal,
Garble a name we detest, and for prejudice?
Set loose the whole consummate pack to bay like Sir Roger de Coverley's

This our reward for our works, sic crescit gloria mundi:
Some circle of not more than three that we prefer to play up to,

Some few whom we'd rather please than hear the whole aegrum vulgrus
Splitting its beery jowl a-meaowling our praises.

Some certain peculiar things, cari laresque, penates,
Some certain accustomed forms, the absolute unimportant.

XII

(AU JARDIN)

O You away high there, you that lean
From amber lattices upon the cobalt night,
I am below amid the pine trees,
Amid the little pine trees, hear me!

"The jester walked in the garden."
Did he so?
Well, there's no use your loving me
That way, Lady;
For I've nothing but songs to give you.

I am set wide upon the world's ways
To say that life is, some way, a gay thing,
But you never string two days upon one wire
But there'll come sorrow of it.
And I loved a love once,

Over beyond the moon there,
I loved a love once,
And, may be, more times,

But she danced like a pink moth in the shrubbery.

Oh, I know you women from the "other folk,"
And it'll all come right,
O' Sundays.

"The jester walked in the garden."
Did he so?

RIPOSTES OF EZRA POUND

Gird on thy star, We'll have this out with fate

TO
WILLIAM CARLOS WILLIAMS

RIPOSTES

SILET

When I behold how black, immortal ink
Drips from my deathless pen—ah, well-away!
Why should we stop at all for what I think?
There is enough in what I chance to say.

It is enough that we once came together;
What is the use of setting it to rime?
When it is autumn do we get spring weather,
Or gather may of harsh northwindish time?

It is enough that we once came together;
What if the wind have turned against the rain?
It is enough that we once came together;
Time has seen this, and will not turn again;

And who are we, who know that last intent,
To plague to-morrow with a testament!

IN EXITUM CUIUSDAM

On a certain one's departure

"Time's bitter flood"! Oh, that's all very well,
But where's the old friend hasn't fallen off,
Or slacked his hand-grip when you first gripped fame?

I know your circle and can fairly tell
What you have kept and what you've left behind:
I know my circle and know very well
How many faces I'd have out of mind.

APPARUIT

Golden rose the house, in the portal I saw
thee, a marvel, carven in subtle stuff, a portent.
Life died down in the lamp and flickered,
caught at the wonder.

Crimson, frosty with dew, the roses bend where
thou afar moving in the glamorous sun
drinkst in life of earth, of the air, the tissue
golden about thee.

Green the ways, the breath of the fields is thine there,
open lies the land, yet the steely going
darkly hast thou dared and the dreaded æther
parted before thee.

Swift at courage thou in the shell of gold, casting
a-loose the cloak of the body, camest
straight, then shone thine oriel and the stunned light
faded about thee.

Half the graven shoulder, the throat aflash with
strands of light inwoven about it, loveliest
of all things, frail alabaster, ah me!
swift in departing,

Clothed in goldish weft, delicately perfect,
gone as wind! The cloth of the magical hands!
Thou a slight thing, thou in access of cunning
dar'dst to assume this?

THE TOMB AT AKR ÇAAR

"I am thy soul, Nikoptis. I have watched
These five millennia, and thy dead eyes
Moved not, nor ever answer my desire,
And thy light limbs, wherethrough I leapt aflame,
Burn not with me nor any saffron thing.

See, the light grass sprang up to pillow thee,
And kissed thee with a myriad grassy tongues;
But not thou me.

I have read out the gold upon the wall,
And wearied out my thought upon the signs.
And there is no new thing in all this place.

I have been kind. See, I have left the jars sealed,
Lest thou shouldst wake and whimper for thy wine.
And all thy robes I have kept smooth on thee.

O thou unmindful! How should I forget!
—Even the river many days ago,
The river, thou wast over young.
And three souls came upon Thee—

And I came.
And I flowed in upon thee, beat them off;
I have been intimate with thee, known thy ways.
Have I not touched thy palms and finger-tips,
Flowed in, and through thee and about thy heels?
How 'came I in'? Was I not thee and Thee?

And no sun comes to rest me in this place,
And I am torn against the jagged dark,
And no light beats upon me, and you say
No word, day after day.

Oh! I could get me out, despite the marks
And all their crafty work upon the door,
Out through the glass-green fields....
*   *   *   *   *
Yet it is quiet here:
I do not go."

PORTRAIT D'UNE FEMME

Your mind and you are our Sargasso Sea,
London has swept about you this score years
And bright ships left you this or that in fee:
Ideas, old gossip, oddments of all things,
Strange spars of knowledge and dimmed wares of price.
Great minds have sought you—lacking someone else.
You have been second always. Tragical?
No. You preferred it to the usual thing:
One dull man, dulling and uxorious,
One average mind—with one thought less, each year.
Oh, you are patient, I have seen you sit
Hours, where something might have floated up.
And now you pay one. Yes, you richly pay.
You are a person of some interest, one comes to you
And takes strange gain away:
Trophies fished up; some curious suggestion;
Fact that leads nowhere; and a tale for two,
Pregnant with mandrakes, or with something else
That might prove useful and yet never proves,
That never fits a corner or shows use,
Or finds its hour upon the loom of days:
The tarnished, gaudy, wonderful old work;
Idols and ambergris and rare inlays,
These are your riches, your great store; and yet
For all this sea-hoard of deciduous things,
Strange woods half sodden, and new brighter stuff:
In the slow float of differing light and deep,
No! there is nothing! In the whole and all,
Nothing that's quite your own.
Yet this is you.

N.Y.

My City, my beloved, my white!
Ah, slender,
Listen! Listen to me, and I will breathe into thee a soul.
Delicately upon the reed, attend me!

Now do I know that I am mad,
For here are a million people surly with traffic;
This is no maid.
Neither could I play upon any reed if I had one.

My City, my beloved,
Thou art a maid with no breasts,
Thou art slender as a silver reed.
Listen to me, attend me!
And I will breathe into thee a soul,
And thou shalt live for ever.

A GIRL

The tree has entered my hands,
The sap has ascended my arms,
The tree has grown in my breast—
Downward,
The branches grow out of me, like arms.

Tree you are,
Moss you are,
You are violets with wind above them.
A child—*so* high—you are,
And all this is folly to the world.

"PHASELLUS ILLE"

This *papier-mâché*, which you see, my friends,
Saith 'twas the worthiest of editors.
Its mind was made up in "the seventies,"
Nor hath it ever since changed that concoction.
It works to represent that school of thought
Which brought the hair-cloth chair to such perfection,
Nor will the horrid threats of Bernard Shaw
Shake up the stagnant pool of its convictions;
Nay, should the deathless voice of all the world
Speak once again for its sole stimulation,
'Twould not move it one jot from left to right.

Come Beauty barefoot from the Cyclades,
She'd find a model for St Anthony
In this thing's sure *decorum* and behaviour.

AN OBJECT

This thing, that hath a code and not a core,
  Hath set acquaintance where might be affections,
And nothing now
Disturbeth his reflections.

QUIES

This is another of our ancient loves.
Pass and be silent, Rullus, for the day
Hath lacked a something since this lady passed;
Hath lacked a something. 'Twas but marginal.

THE SEAFARER

(*From the early Anglo-Saxon text*)

May I for my own self song's truth reckon,
Journey's jargon, how I in harsh days
Hardship endured oft.
Bitter breast-cares have I abided,
Known on my keel many a care's hold,
And dire sea-surge, and there I oft spent
Narrow nightwatch nigh the ship's head
While she tossed close to cliffs. Coldly afflicted,
My feet were by frost benumbed.
Chill its chains are; chafing sighs
Hew my heart round and hunger begot
Mere-weary mood. Lest man know not
That he on dry land loveliest liveth,
List how I, care-wretched, on ice-cold sea,
Weathered the winter, wretched outcast
Deprived of my kinsmen;
Hung with hard ice-flakes, where hail-scur flew,
There I heard naught save the harsh sea
And ice-cold wave, at whiles the swan cries,
Did for my games the gannet's clamour,
Sea-fowls' loudness was for me laughter,
The mews' singing all my mead-drink.
Storms, on the stone-cliffs beaten, fell on the stern
In icy feathers; full oft the eagle screamed
With spray on his pinion.
Not any protector
May make merry man faring needy.
This he little believes, who aye in winsome life
Abides 'mid burghers some heavy business,
Wealthy and wine-flushed, how I weary oft
Must bide above brine.
Neareth nightshade, snoweth from north,
Frost froze the land, hail fell on earth then
Corn of the coldest. Nathless there knocketh now
The heart's thought that I on high streams
The salt-wavy tumult traverse alone.

Moaneth alway my mind's lust
That I fare forth, that I afar hence
Seek out a foreign fastness.
For this there's no mood-lofty man over earth's midst,
Not though he be given his good, but will have in his youth greed;
Nor his deed to the daring, nor his king to the faithful
But shall have his sorrow for sea-fare
Whatever his lord will.
He hath not heart for harping, nor in ring-having
Nor winsomeness to wife, nor world's delight
Nor any whit else save the wave's slash,
Yet longing comes upon him to fare forth on the water.
Bosque taketh blossom, cometh beauty of berries,
Fields to fairness, land fares brisker,
All this admonisheth man eager of mood,
The heart turns to travel so that he then thinks
On flood-ways to be far departing.
Cuckoo calleth with gloomy crying,
He singeth summerward, bodeth sorrow,
The bitter heart's blood. Burgher knows not—
He the prosperous man—what some perform
Where wandering them widest draweth.
So that but now my heart burst from my breast-lock,
My mood 'mid the mere-flood,
Over the whale's acre, would wander wide.
On earth's shelter cometh oft to me,
Eager and ready, the crying lone-flyer,
Whets for the whale-path the heart irresistibly,
O'er tracks of ocean; seeing that anyhow
My lord deems to me this dead life
On loan and on land, I believe not
That any earth-weal eternal standeth
Save there be somewhat calamitous
That, ere a man's tide go, turn it to twain.
Disease or oldness or sword-hate
Beats out the breath from doom-gripped body.
And for this, every earl whatever, for those speaking after—
Laud of the living, boasteth some last word,
That he will work ere he pass onward,
Frame on the fair earth 'gainst foes his malice,
Daring ado,...
So that all men shall honour him after
And his laud beyond them remain 'mid the English,
Aye, for ever, a lasting life's-blast,
Delight mid the doughty.
Days little durable,

And all arrogance of earthen riches,
There come now no kings nor Cæsars
Nor gold-giving lords like those gone.
Howe'er in mirth most magnified,
Whoe'er lived in life most lordliest,
Drear all this excellence, delights undurable!
Waneth the watch, but the world holdeth.
Tomb hideth trouble. The blade is layed low.
Earthly glory ageth and seareth.
No man at all going the earth's gait,
But age fares against him, his face paleth,
Grey-haired he groaneth, knows gone companions,
Lordly men are to earth o'ergiven,
Nor may he then the flesh-cover, whose life ceaseth,
Nor eat the sweet nor feel the sorry,
Nor stir hand nor think in mid heart,
And though he strew the grave with gold,
His born brothers, their buried bodies
Be an unlikely treasure hoard.

ECHOES

I

GUIDO ORLANDO, SINGING

Befits me praise thine empery,
Lady of Valour,
Past all disproving;
Thou art the flower to me—
Nay, by Love's pallor—
Of all good loving.

Worthy to reap men's praises
Is he who'd gaze upon
Truth's mazes.
In like commend is he,
Who, loving fixedly,
Love so refineth,

Till thou alone art she
In whom love's vested;
As branch hath fairest flower
Where fruit's suggested.

This great joy comes to me,
To me observing
How swiftly thou hast power
To pay my serving.

II[1]

Thou keep'st thy rose-leaf
Till the rose-time will be over,
Think'st thou that Death will kiss thee?
Think'st thou that the Dark House
Will find thee such a lover
As I? Will the new roses miss thee?

Prefer my cloak unto the cloak of dust
'Neath which the last year lies,
For thou shouldst more mistrust

---

[1] Asclepiades, Julianus Ægyptus.

Time than my eyes.

AN IMMORALITY

Sing we for love and idleness,
Naught else is worth the having.

Though I have been in many a land,
There is naught else in living.

And I would rather have my sweet,
Though rose-leaves die of grieving,

Than do high deeds in Hungary
To pass all men's believing.

DIEU! QU'IL LA FAIT

From Charles D'Orleans
For music

God! that mad'st her well regard her,
How she is so fair and bonny;
For the great charms that are upon her
Ready are all folk to reward her.

Who could part him from her borders
When spells are alway renewed on her?
God! that mad'st her well regard her,
How she is so fair and bonny.

From here to there to the sea's border,
Dame nor damsel there's not any
Hath of perfect charms so many.
Thoughts of her are of dream's order:
God! that mad'st her well regard her.

SALVE PONTIFEX

(A.C.S.)

One after one they leave thee,
High Priest of Iacchus,
Intoning thy melodies as winds intone
The whisperings of leaves on sunlit days.
And the sands are many
And the seas beyond the sands are one
In ultimate, so we here being many
Are unity; nathless thy compeers,
Knowing thy melody,
Lulled with the wine of thy music
Go seaward silently, leaving thee sentinel
O'er all the mysteries,
High Priest of Iacchus.
For the lines of life lie under thy fingers,
And above the vari-coloured strands
Thine eyes look out unto the infinitude
Of the blue waves of heaven,
And even as Triplex Sisterhood
Thou fingerest the threads knowing neither
Cause nor the ending,
High Priest of Iacchus,
Draw'st forth a multiplicity
Of strands, and, beholding
The colour thereof, raisest thy voice
Towards the sunset,
O High Priest of Iacchus!
And out of the secrets of the inmost mysteries
Thou chantest strange far-sourced canticles:
O High Priest of Iacchus!
Life and the ways of Death her
Twin-born sister, that is life's counterpart,
And of night and the winds of night;
Silent voices ministering to the souls
Of hamadryads that hold council concealèd
In streams and tree-shadowing

Forests on hill slopes,
O High Priest of Iacchus,
All the manifold mystery
Thou makest a wine of song,
And maddest thy following even
With visions of great deeds
And their futility,
O High Priest of Iacchus!
Though thy co-novices are bent to the scythe
Of the magian wind that is voice of Persephone,
Leaving thee solitary, master of initiating
Mænads that come through the
Vine-entangled ways of the forest
Seeking, out of all the world,
Madness of Iacchus,
That being skilled in the secrets of the double cup
They might turn the dead of the world
Into pæans,
O High Priest of Iacchus,
Wreathed with the glory of thy years of creating
Entangled music,
Breathe!
Now that the evening cometh upon thee,
Breathe upon us, that low-bowed and exultant
Drink wine of Iacchus, that since the conquering
Hath been chiefly containèd in the numbers
Of them that, even as thou, have woven
Wicker baskets for grape clusters
Wherein is concealèd the source of the vintage,
O High Priest of Iacchus,
Breathe thou upon us
Thy magic in parting!
Even as they thy co-novices,
At being mingled with the sea,
While yet thou madest thy canticles
Serving upright before the altar
That is bound about with shadows
Of dead years wherein thy Iacchus
Looked not upon the hills, that being
Uncared for, praised not him in entirety.
O High Priest of Iacchus,
Being now near to the border of the sands
Where the sapphire girdle of the sea
Encinctureth the maiden
Persephone, released for the spring,
Look! Breathe upon us

The wonder of the thrice encinctured mystery
Whereby thou being full of years art young,
Loving even this lithe Persephone
That is free for the seasons of plenty;
Whereby thou being young art old
And shalt stand before this Persephone
Whom thou lovest,
In darkness, even at that time
That she being returned to her husband
Shall be queen and a maiden no longer,
Wherein thou being neither old nor young
Standing on the verge of the sea
Shalt pass from being sand,
O High Priest of Iacchus,
And becoming wave
Shalt encircle all sands,
Being transmuted through all
The girdling of the sea.

O High Priest of Iacchus,
Breathe thou upon us!

    Note.—This apostrophe was written three years before Swinburne's death.

Δώρια

B e in me as the eternal moods of the bleak wind, and not
As transient things are—gaiety of flowers.
Have me in the strong loneliness of sunless cliffs
And of grey waters.
Let the gods speak softly of us
In days hereafter,
The shadowy flowers of Orcus
Remember Thee.

THE NEEDLE

Come, or the stellar tide will slip away,
Eastward avoid the hour of its decline,
Now! for the needle trembles in my soul!

Here have we had our vantage, the good hour.
Here we have had our day, your day and mine.
Come now, before this power
That bears us up, shall turn against the pole.

Mock not the flood of stars, the thing's to be.
O Love, come now, this land turns evil slowly.
The waves bore in, soon will they bear away.

The treasure is ours, make we fast land with it.
Move we and take the tide, with its next favour,
Abide
Under some neutral force
Until this course turneth aside.

SUB MARE

It is, and is not, I am sane enough,
Since you have come this place has hovered round me,
This fabrication built of autumn roses,
Then there's a goldish colour, different.

And one gropes in these things as delicate
Algae reach up and out beneath
Pale slow green surgings of the under-wave,
'Mid these things older than the names they have,
These things that are familiars of the god.

PLUNGE

I would bathe myself in strangeness:
These comforts heaped upon me, smother me!
I burn, I scald so for the new,
New friends, new faces,
Places!
Oh to be out of this,
This that is all I wanted
—save the new.
And you,
Love, you the much, the more desired!
Do I not loathe all walls, streets, stones,
All mire, mist, all fog,
All ways of traffic?
You, I would have flow over me like water,
Oh, but far out of this!
Grass, and low fields, and hills,
And sun,
Oh, sun enough!
Out and alone, among some
Alien people!

A VIRGINAL

No, no! Go from me. I have left her lately,
I will not spoil my sheath with lesser brightness,
For my surrounding air has a new lightness;
Slight are her arms, yet they have bound me straitly
And left me cloaked as with a gauze of æther;
As with sweet leaves; as with a subtle clearness.
Oh, I have picked up magic in her nearness
To sheathe me half in half the things that sheathe her.

No, no! Go from me. I have still the flavour,
Soft as spring wind that's come from birchen bowers.
Green come the shoots, aye April in the branches,
As winter's wound with her sleight hand she staunches,
Hath of the tress a likeness of the savour:
As white their bark, so white this lady's hours.

PAN IS DEAD

Pan is dead. Great Pan is dead.
  Ah! bow your heads, ye maidens all,
And weave ye him his coronal.

There is no summer in the leaves,
And withered are the sedges;
How shall we weave a coronal,
Or gather floral pledges?

That I may not say, Ladies.
Death was ever a churl.
That I may not say, Ladies.
How should he show a reason,
That he has taken our Lord away
Upon such hollow season?

THE PICTURE[2]

The eyes of this dead lady speak to me,
For here was love, was not to be drowned out,
And here desire, not to be kissed away.

The eyes of this dead lady speak to me.

[2] "Venus Reclining," by Jacopo del Sellaio (1442-93).

OF JACOPO DEL SELLAIO

This man knew out the secret ways of love,
No man could paint such things who did not know.

And now she's gone, who was his Cyprian,
And you are here, who are "The Isles" to me.

And here's the thing that lasts the whole thing out:
The eyes of this dead lady speak to me.

THE RETURN

See, they return; ah, see the tentative
Movements, and the slow feet,
The trouble in the pace and the uncertain
Wavering!

See, they return, one, and by one,
With fear, as half-awakened;
As if the snow should hesitate
And murmur in the wind, and half turn back;
These were the "Wing'd-with-Awe,"
Inviolable.

Gods of the wingèd shoe!
With them the silver hounds, sniffing the trace of air!

Haie! Haie!
These were the swift to harry;
These the keen-scented;
These were the souls of blood.

Slow on the leash, pallid the leash-men.

EFFECTS OF MUSIC UPON A COMPANY OF PEOPLE

I

DEUX MOVEMENTS

1. Temple qui fut.

2. Poissons d'or.

1

A soul curls back,
Their souls like petals,
Thin, long, spiral,
Like those of a chrysanthemum curl
Smoke-like up and back from the
Vavicel, the calyx,
Pale green, pale gold, transparent,
Green of plasma, rose-white,
Spirate like smoke,
Curled,
Vibrating,
Slowly, waving slowly.
O Flower animate!
O calyx!
O crowd of foolish people!

2

The petals!
On the tip of each the figure
Delicate.
See, they dance, step to step.
Flora to festival,
Twine, bend, bow,
Frolic involve ye.
Woven the step,
Woven the tread, the moving.
Ribands they move,

Wave, bow to the centre.
Pause, rise, deepen in colour,
And fold in drowsily.

II
FROM A THING BY SCHUMANN

Breast high, floating and welling
Their soul, moving beneath the satin,
Plied the gold threads,
Pushed at the gauze above it.
The notes beat upon this,
Beat and indented it;
Rain dropped and came and fell upon this,
Hail and snow,
My sight gone in the flurry!

And then across the white silken,
Bellied up, as a sail bellies to the wind,
Over the fluid tenuous, diaphanous,
Over this curled a wave, greenish,
Mounted and overwhelmed it.
This membrane floating above,
And bellied out by the up-pressing soul.

Then came a mer-host,
And after them legion of Romans,
The usual, dull, theatrical!

THE COMPLETE POETICAL WORKS
OF T.E. HULME

PREFATORY NOTE

In publishing his *Complete Poetical Works* at thirty,[3] Mr Hulme has set an enviable example to many of his contemporarieswho have had less to say.

They are reprinted here for good fellowship; for good custom, a custom out of Tuscany and of Provence; and thirdly, for convenience, seeing their smallness of bulk; and for good memory, seeing that they recall certain evenings and meetings of two years gone, dull enough at the time, but rather pleasant to look back upon.

As for the "School of Images," which may or may not have existed, its principles were not so interesting as those of the "inherent dynamists" or of *Les Unanimistes*, yet they were probably sounder than those of a certain French school which attempted to dispense with verbs altogether; or of the Impressionists who brought forth:

"Pink pigs blossoming upon the hillside";

or of the Post-Impressionists who beseech their ladies to let down slate-blue hair over their raspberry-coloured flanks.

Ardoise rimed richly—ah, richly and rarely rimed!—with *framboise*.

As for the future, *Les Imagistes*, the descendants of the forgotten school of 1909, have that in their keeping.

I refrain from publishing my proposed *Historical Memoir* of their forerunners, because Mr Hulme has threatened to print the original propaganda.

E.P.

---

[3] Mr Pound has grossly exaggerated my age.—T.E.H.

AUTUMN

A touch of cold in the Autumn night—
I walked abroad,
And saw the ruddy moon lean over a hedge
Like a red-faced farmer.
I did not stop to speak, but nodded,
And round about were the wistful stars
With white faces like town children.

MANA ABODA

Beauty is the marking-time, the stationary vibration, the feigned ecstasy of an arrested impulse unable to reach its natural end.

Mana Aboda, whose bent form
The sky in archèd circle is,
Seems ever for an unknown grief to mourn.
Yet on a day I heard her cry:
"I weary of the roses and the singing poets—
Josephs all, not tall enough to try."

ABOVE THE DOCK

Above the quiet dock in mid night,
Tangled in the tall mast's corded height,
Hangs the moon. What seemed so far away
Is but a child's balloon, forgotten after play.

THE EMBANKMENT

(The fantasia of a fallen gentleman on a cold, bitter night.)

Once, in finesse of fiddles found I ecstasy,
In the flash of gold heels on the hard pavement.
Now see I
That warmth's the very stuff of poesy.
Oh, God, make small
The old star-eaten blanket of the sky,
That I may fold it round me and in comfort lie.

CONVERSION

Lighthearted I walked into the valley wood
In the time of hyacinths,
Till beauty like a scented cloth
Cast over, stifled me. I was bound
Motionless and faint of breath
By loveliness that is her own eunuch.

Now pass I to the final river
Ignominiously, in a sack, without sound,
As any peeping Turk to the Bosphorus.

FINIS

Lector House believes that a society develops through a two-fold approach of continuous learning and adaptation, which is derived from the study of classic literary works spread across the historic timeline of literature records. Therefore, we aim at reviving, repairing and redeveloping all those inaccessible or damaged but historically as well as culturally important literature across subjects so that the future generations may have an opportunity to study and learn from past works to embark upon a journey of creating a better future.

This book is a result of an effort made by Lector House towards making a contribution to the preservation and repair of original ancient works which might hold historical significance to the approach of continuous learning across subjects.

HAPPY READING & LEARNING!

LECTOR HOUSE
LECTOR HOUSE LLP
E-MAIL: lectorpublishing@gmail.com